MW01608554

Hornets

An Educational Children's Book about Hornets with Fun Facts & Photos

Abby Daniele

I am a hornet.

I am an insect.

I only attack when I feel like I'm in danger.

I like building my nest in high places.

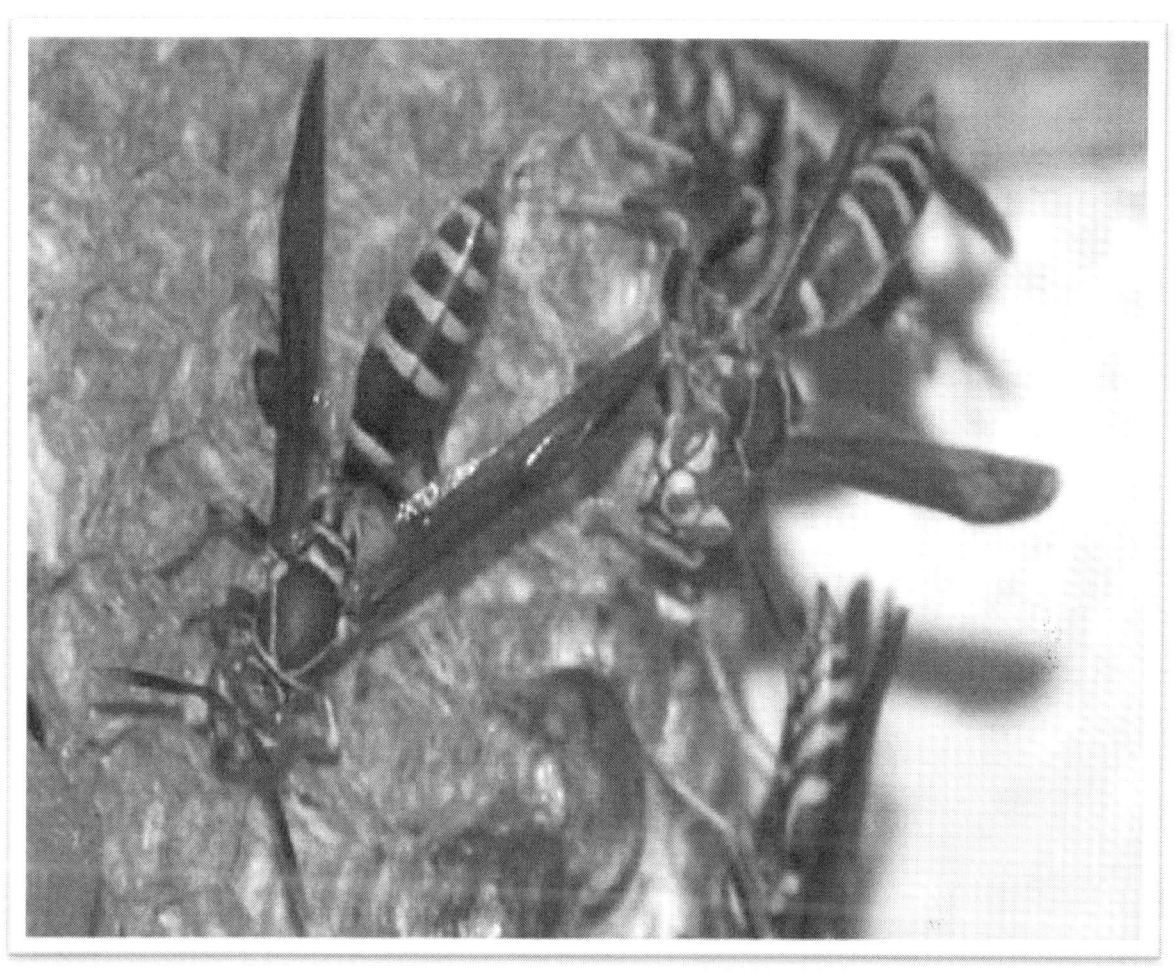

I'm a gardener's friend because I eat smaller insects and pests.

Just like you, I love sweet stuff!

I love bees because they give me protein and they have honey hidden in their hives. ✗

My sting contains venom that can be very dangerous and deadly.

I have two pairs of wings.

We hornets don't live very long. ✗

We die after a year and only the next queens survive.

We can be striped yellow and black but sometimes, we are also colored red orange.

Only our queen can lay eggs.

We build our nests out of chewed wood mixed with our saliva.

We like looking for food at night.

Our eggs take only 5 to 8 days to hatch.

To start a colony, our queen starts building the nest and laying eggs.

When eggs grow into worker hornets, they take over building and looking for food to feed the larvae.

There are about 500 of us in one nest!

When in danger, I can call my other friends to defend the whole nest.

All hornet workers are females.

We build our nests on branches, inside tree hollows, and even in attics.

Made in the USA
San Bernardino, CA
28 May 2019